THE COMMUNICATION CODE

*Relational selling secrets
to boost your sales*

by

Steven Wener

©2019 by Steven Wener

Intelligent Life Books

TABLE OF CONTENTS

INTRODUCTION

You've made a really smart move picking up this book. This guide is your unique opportunity to become an exceptional sales person and propel your career toward success. I've been blessed to have learned several key strategies that have helped me to multiply my sales by unleashing the power of communication. The simple-yet-powerful strategies I explain in this book have the potential to truly change your life!

For an introduction to the importance of clear communication, read this sentence:

Welcome to a yoeunjr that si mitsselli ni brinigng both ppyioortuiyn adn growht.

I'm sure you'll agree these jumbled spellings are an editor's nightmare! Perhaps you figured out the sentence fairly quickly, or maybe you're still struggling to decode the words. Let's unscramble the sentence:

Welcome to a journey that is limitless in bringing both opportunity and growth.

If something can't be clearly understood, how effective is the message? That's the question you must ask yourself before pitching a product, a solution, or yourself.

In both your verbal and written communications, your customers must have a clear understanding of the message. Ineffective communication is like your GPS taking you to the wrong location, or paying for merchandise with cash and getting short-changed — unfulfilled expectations can be frustrating, and derail your goals. This book provides you a formula for effective communication that will get you and your customers to your desired destinations.

As you learn the fundamentals of effective communication, you'll begin to experience more engaging conversations, find incredible opportunities, develop new friendships, and experience substantial growth in both your professional and personal life.

These results don't come from taking a magic pill; it takes dedication and work. The juice is in the squeeze — you need to play with the techniques in this book and put them into practice. Over time, you'll see the puzzle pieces come together beautifully — and you'll never be the same!

My hope is that you'll be encouraged to take the steps necessary to begin your own personal journey to fulfill your greatest potential. If I have been able to play even a small part in your journey, then I'm fulfilled by living out part of my true purpose!

A Diamond in the Rough

From a young age, I've had the ability to connect with others on a deeper level; I am very grateful for that gift. I'm sure you have a set of natural gifts of your own — gifts that I do *not* have! Each one of us is gifted with our own set of talents and aptitudes, but few of us make the effort to effectively turn those talents and aptitudes into polished and productive skills for the benefit of ourselves and others.

Consider a diamond — a rare and precious stone renowned for its beauty and value. Imagine the thrill and anticipation a diamond cutter must feel when he first lays hands on an unusually large, raw diamond. He instinctively knows its incredible potential as he visualizes the end product in his mind's eye. From this vantage point, he sees an exquisite, chiseled diamond being placed on the finger of an awe-struck, overwhelmingly grateful recipient.

Think about the process that begins with the raw stone in the hands of this seasoned professional stonecutter. Utilizing an eye piece, he holds the precious stone up to the light. He rotates it in every direction possible, closely inspecting each minute angle and reflection. This initial inspection provides him with a clear understanding of the stone's true array of colors and genuine potential. Next, he creates a 3D model of the raw stone. This model will reveal every imperfection, assisting him in the process of *planning*. These steps are critical to determine the number of separate stones that can come from the one diamond, possible shapes that can be hewn, and of course, the carat weight.

The next step necessary for the stone to reach its full potential is probably the toughest, as well as the most important step of all: a process call *cleaving* or *sawing* — effectively removing each unnecessary or undesirable part of the rough diamond. This is a lot like the process of personal growth: you have to identify, then unreservedly cleave away, each unproductive habit or hindering belief — one by one — not an easy or pleasant process! However, with each pass at the diamond, the cutter gets closer and closer to shaping the rough diamond into its utmost resplendent form. This tough process is necessary for each one of us as we seek to hone and maximize our raw gifts to reach our goals.

The next process is called bruting: the diamond is placed on a spinning axle, along with special diamond-coated surfaces that turn in opposite directions for the purpose of grinding the diamond down, so it can be shaped to perfection. The journey to unlocking our full potential is generally not easy, but it's essential and purposeful. It's in the grind of our life experiences and personal interactions that we each are set on our own unique journey that will ultimately unleash this full potential, allowing us to reach ultimate success.

Now that the diamonds have been shaped, it's time for the polish. This buffing brings out the brilliance and individuality of the diamond. This is the crowning process of making a diamond — the one distinctive stone renowned and admired for its timeless beauty, color, and shape. As you can see, the end product did not create itself; it was crafted by seasoned, skilled hands through a time-honored, specific and methodical process. Should our personal shaping be any less?

In the world of sales, there's really no higher goal and joy than having potential clients genuinely focus on what you're saying, desire to actively follow your advice, and ultimately decide that you're the person they choose to work with. Take a moment to envision this new life — a life in which you're rewarded with these results on a regular basis. Wouldn't that be revolutionary and fulfilling?

But what keeps us from arriving at this desirable outcome naturally? We tend to underestimate the power of our words, the importance of our body language, and the pronounced impact of our voice — our tonality, inflection and cadence. Learning how to use all of these communication styles will help you chisel off your rough spots and bring you closer to your desired outcome.

When Life Hands You Lemons...

Now, let's begin your process. In your mind, imagine the best scenario. Imagine you and your product being enthusiastically received with heightened interest and considerable esteem. Try to envision the setting where this is taking place.

- What are you wearing?
- How are you expressing yourself and what are you saying?
- What are the facial expressions and body language responses of those listening to you?

Take a few moments to allow the communications, the emotions, and the fulfillment of that encounter to submerge your thoughts to the core of your very being. This preliminary "visual" understanding is the beginning of your future success. You have now officially started the process of becoming a champion — in your own mind. From this moment on, you'll discover that one success will build upon another until success becomes the norm, rather than the exception.

I want to share with you an example of the power of your mind. Imagine a lemon for a moment — not just any lemon, but a big, fat, juicy, plump lemon, hanging low on a branch. If you love lemons as I do, the scent is so irresistible, you just have to have a bite! So, you pluck it from the tree, bring it up to your nose, and inhale its overwhelming aroma. Can you smell that? Now you sink your teeth into its rind and savor the juice as it lands on your taste buds. You can't wait for your next bite! Now, as you were envisioning this scenario, did you begin to salivate like I did? In all likelihood, you did. We all know from experience that our senses can respond to vivid pictures in our minds; this is called the mind-body connection. You don't need to have the physical lemon in your hand to salivate!

In the same way, your mind and physical body can envision success, as well as each step of the path that will you lead you to that success. This is how you begin your *new normal* — this is how you begin to change your thought patterns and your patterns of success. This book is all about change and new habit formation. However, it cannot be overstated that change takes time. We all wish we could change with the snap of a finger! But that's not reality; let's reel in our expectations and take a realistic look at this life-changing process.

How many times have you come back from a conference all fired up with new, awesome ideas to create amazing and lasting change? You put into practice everything you just heard, you see some positive change, but a few weeks down the road you hit a brick wall.

The changes didn't stick — you're back to your old ways, and you're really bummed! Please hear me: it doesn't have to be that way! When you understand the science of learning and how your brain works, and you actually put it into practice, success is just around the corner.

If you're over the age of twenty-five, this change will take some more work. Our brains solidify as we age, which causes our neuropathways to become deeply rooted. Our brains want to follow the path of least resistance, the old patterns of familiarity. The good news is, you can build new neuropathways! It just takes time, effort, and consistency. You can expect it to take a minimum of three months of being immersed in working your new plan to build those brand new neuropathways.

The Value of Verbal

One of the biggest challenges we face today is living in a society built around immediate gratification. Technology has been a game changer for innovation and efficiency, making always-on communication quick and easy; unfortunately, technology has also negatively impacted our work ethic. Studies show that Millennials generally have a significantly reduced work ethic when compared to older generations. Working hard to "win the prize" is a dying art. Our cell phones have become appendages to our bodies. Over

90% of all text messages sent are read within the first three minutes![1] While that may indicate efficiency, it comes at a cost. As a society, we no longer know how to wait, work, and persevere — or how to stay focused on a task without distractions.

I recently read an article about how texting impacts the communication dynamic for both the sender and the receiver of messages. It noted that sometimes people will send a text ahead of a call, so the recipient knows they're about to call, or to try to avoid a call altogether and just take care of the issue via text.[2] The simple act of texting ahead of a call can actually trigger anxiety for the recipient, because normally the two parties just text instead of calling. So, the first thought the recipient has is, "They're calling! There must be something wrong!" Now, that mindset sounds crazy to me, because I don't live in a text-only world — I'm a "phone call first" kind of guy as much as possible, as that's my preferred method of communicating. Sure, I embrace texting and email — both certainly have their place — but they always feel less personal to me. The article concluded by announcing that "the phone is back" (meaning calling rather than texting). Yes, people are actually starting to recognize the value of a phone call over a mere text or email. This is important, because the easiest channel of communication is not always the best, and you have to be the best if you want to succeed.

Ultimately, technology changes, and will always change — but true principles don't. At a young age, I worked with my dad, and he always had a pocket full of quarters. This was just in case his pager went off and he had to find a payphone to make a sales-related call. Then, he graduated to a car phone, and eventually to the first handheld wireless phone (nicknamed "the brick" — you could single-handedly win a bar fight with one of those big, bulky monsters). He never did build a company website or get into technology, he just made his calls and set appointments regardless of what kind of phone he was using.

CHAPTER 1

WE ALL HAVE A STORY — HERE'S MINE

As long as we're taking a stroll down memory lane, I'd like to take a moment to explain my background, so you have an understanding of my credentials as a communication expert, and how I developed the steps you'll learn in this book.

I was born in Montreal, Quebec, Canada, in a very tight family that was full of love. As a child, we spent most of our time at my grandmother's house (and so did the rest of the neighborhood, it seemed). I'm the oldest of three, and my mother, Esther, is the oldest of ten. I was constantly surrounded by my aunts, uncles, cousins, and family friends, and the front door to Grandma's was always open. The ten-by-ten kitchen was the focal point of our gatherings. With Mom's side from Morocco, there was a never-ending flow of mint tea, café-au-lait, homemade cookies and bread, card games with constant cheating, screaming the loudest to be heard over everybody else, constant laughing, and cigarette smoke that could rival the thickest smoke from a fire. I loved every minute of it, and it prepared me from the beginning to be accustomed to all kinds of people. There were loud people, funny people, talented people, comedians, great cooks, helpful people, and lazy people. Regardless of who you were, there was room for you, no matter how full the kitchen...but if I wanted to be heard, I had to be the loudest of the bunch. Now, I know all families aren't built this way, so this is why I want to preface my story; it wasn't a quiet, sit down style of family where manners and being appropriate are paramount. My younger days were chaotic, fun, and full of life.

Then there was my father — a true salesman's salesman. He was part-owner of a home renovation business, and his personality — which was very strong and direct — coupled with living in my grandmother's kitchen environment, truly shaped me. Dad was super old-school sales. He hated wasting time, and he sold strictly business to consumer. To make a living, he commuted from Montreal to Ottawa, and was gone from Monday to Thursday every week for years. Dad worked incredibly hard, and sacrificed time with us in order to provide for us financially. I can't imagine how hard that was, so thank you, Dad!

Fast forward a few years to my early twenties when I was freshly armed with a real estate license, and it was time to find my first brokerage. I interviewed at Royal Le Page, a national real estate chain. I'll never forget being interviewed by the broker, Judy. She put me through a rigorous test called the mirror test: if I could fog a mirror, she'd hire me. Yep...not much of a barrier to entry in real estate, and not much has changed in over twenty years!

So, now I had a license and an office to work from — what to do next? Does this sound familiar to you, regardless of the industry you're in? Thankfully, I had some experience in how to hustle, and understood the ways my father successfully grew his business. First step: get your name out there!

In real estate you hear about *farming*, or sending direct mail pieces to a geographic area over and over again, until the neighborhood becomes familiar with you, and prospective clients call you when they're in need of your services. Well, my dad was essentially farming before it was a thing. He would also advertise in the yellow pages, the internet of Dad's time. His reviews came in the form of the Better Business Bureau, or BBB. He was a long-term member with the BBB, and would always let prospective clients know that he was in excellent standing with BBB — the *gold standard* when it came to consumer confidence.

For me, I found door knocking to be an excellent way to make an impression. I learned door knocking skills from my childhood experiences going out with Dad in the still-light late evenings of the Edmonton summers, going door to door and developing a work ethic without even realizing it at the time. The experience did teach me a lot about people fairly quickly though, as my father categorized the different types of people he would encounter at the door. He told me I'd meet what he called *strokers*, *brokers*, *lonely people*, and *mooches*.

The stroker is someone who shows interest in your service, but always has some story as to why they can't pull the trigger on moving forward. It's always so close to a sale, but in the end, it never goes anywhere. When you're new, talking to a stroker is actually pretty exciting because you think you may have a sale. Unfortunately, if you don't know how to qualify the lead properly, you keep thinking they may materialize into a sale, and you expend far more energy than needed to keep a follow-up plan going. Better to establish a firm "NO" than to keep getting strung along by a stroker.

The broker is the type of person who never has any money, but they love sharing stories about everything they would like to do if they just had the money. They'll tell you how close they were to hitting the lottery, getting a huge payday at work, that they have a great invention, or whatever else they can dream up — but it's usually all a pipe dream of unrealistic possibilities.

The lonely person is pretty self-explanatory. They are generally the older demographic — likely widowed or living alone, and they don't get many people at their door. I always had a soft spot for the lonely person, because I love human connection so much. They'll invite you in and immediately begin to share stories of a spouse that passed away or how their children don't visit often. They'll take out photos of importance to them, and offer something to eat or drink. In these scenarios, if you don't pay attention to time, you could end up staying a while, and my objective was to find a homeowner who needed work done to their home and to spend time with my dad.

The mooch was the "Holy Grail" of what Dad sought in a homeowner. They had money, their timing was fairly immediate, and they already had an idea of what they wanted to have done to their home. The only thing left for the mooch to do was find a company to hire. And Dad would be right there ready to fill that need.

He was an incredible closer, and once he got in, his success rate was remarkably high. He was a great person to learn from at a young age, and I also got to see how his canvassers worked and what they were looking for before they brought my Dad in for the close.

My father's best canvasser could identify the type of person he was talking to very quickly, and act accordingly: if he could tell from the conversation that there was no potential for a sale, he would just turn away and leave while the person was mid-sentence. I'll never forget the bewildered look on homeowners' faces as he'd walk away. Not my style, but certainly a "no time-wasting" mindset!

Dad was fearless and daring with conversation, so he had a very high close ratio because he had a natural ability to connect. So, when we found a mooch and brought Dad back to the home to meet the owners, it was *show time*. His personality would shift completely, so I could easily detect when he was in "showman" mode — and people would eat it up.

So, how did my first year in real estate go? Taking my experiences from door knocking with Dad, and understanding personality types, I had moderate success, selling ten homes. Not too shabby for a 23-year-old rookie. It felt great to earn real money for the first time, and it's all because I never feared knocking on doors — thanks to spending time with Dad as a kid.

CHAPTER 2

PAINT THEM A PICTURE

"Some men see things as they are, and ask why. I dream of things that never were, and ask why not."
— attr. Robert Kennedy

Without imagination, there would be nothing. Imagination is the key to storytelling.

Let me paint *you* a picture: As language began to develop some 100,000 years ago, envision our ancestors sitting in a cave eating a kill from a hunt, and picture them telling the story of the event. Imagine yourself in the cave as one of the hunters begins moving around the cave with a spear as he's reenacting the event through dance, movement and grunts. Loud grunts when the kill happened and the thrusting of his spear until the animal lay dead. The clan of people can appreciate how the food got to them, and the young boys not old enough to hunt yet have a mental picture of what life will look like for them when they're old enough to join their elders.

In the age before YouTube "how-to" videos, storytelling formed an important part of our instructional experiences. Even as recently as 1820, only 12 percent of the population could read.[3] Today the global literacy rate is 83 percent,[4] and with email and texting, information is instant, abundant, accessible, and we expect answers or replies immediately. Imagine that: back in the not-too-distant past, if you didn't know something, you had to be content with that condition!

The skill of the storyteller has diminished in importance since TV, radio, phones, computers and tablets are there to quench our thirst for breaking news, information about hobbies, education, passions, or anything else we desire to explore. The art of storytelling is gradually being eroded by this seismic shift in society. The demand for immediate answers results in an expectation that we'll "cut to the chase" and skip the journey of discovery. This is a loss for all of us, as storytelling provides greater context, depth of meaning, and personal connection than the mere input-output of a web search on Alexa or Google.

I was speaking with someone in the tech world, and he described how tech work environments are now set up: scores of people all working in a single room, and other than the tapping of the keyboards, you can hear a pin drop. Silence is the norm among these masses of coworkers in these work spaces, and people literally sitting immediately behind a colleague won't step over and start a conversation — instead they'll message them. If they do step over, they whisper so as to not disturb the room. It blows my mind that a personable "talker" like me is becoming more and more of a commodity due to this change in the work environment. The new generation, naturally seeking personal connection, now does so through a keyboard more than ever.

Storytelling is one of the greatest common denominators that binds and defines humanity, as we connect through verbal, emotional and visual cues. *Homo sapiens* may be the only creature on earth that can tell a story through words, gestures, tonality, expression, and can speak the same sentence in a different tone and completely change its meaning.

Of course, technology continues to change the way we tell stories. Look at the impact movies have in our lives since the first public screening of a film took place December 28th, 1895, in Paris. Within a decade, film grew from being a novelty into a serious business, and is of course a huge part of our cultural fabric today.

Film and TV tap in to our imaginations and our very souls, and have shaped the future — all because someone created a way for the masses to experience storytelling. In America, the average adult watches over *five hours* of TV each day. Now with phones, tablets and TVs combined, the average American consumes close to *eleven hours a day* of visual content.

So, who's your favorite onscreen personality, and why? Think about why you connect to that person, as it's an important step into the rest of this chapter. What makes you gravitate towards them (other than them being hot)? Do they appear sincere, sound trustworthy, have relatable mannerisms?

Remember my dad, the salesman? Speaking to prospects, he was always very animated, and he made sure he spoke in visual terms. He explained how the renovations to their home would look, how the changes would ultimately impact their lifestyle, described the updated appearance of the home compared to others in the area, and anything else of relevance. In short, he painted a picture to make them fall in love with what was about to happen. Let me repeat that, because this is the magic: *he made them fall in love with what was about to happen*. I grew up with a storyteller, and didn't fully recognize how most of the world didn't have that advantage.

A *Psychology Today* article called "Learning Through Visuals" describes how visual cues help us better retrieve and remember information, but also connect to it personally.[5] When my dad was in a selling environment, he would use the sample products he kept in the trunk of his car, so he could physically build part of the picture he was painting for the prospective client. He would get them to interact by choosing double or triple pane windows, what color vinyl siding they wanted, and matching the roof shingles to the vinyl color. He helped the client paint the picture themselves as part of the process, giving them ownership in the vision.

By being a story teller, he sold the sizzle. He delivered a front row seat to a movie that entertained the client in such a way that they would gladly pay to see it again, buy the poster and memorabilia, and recommend my father's company to others.

You see, we don't sell a product, we sell *ourselves* as a franchise that people will pay money for — good money — as they will be entertained, taken care of, and leave the show talking about it for hours and sharing it with their friends. In the end, as salespeople, we are actually entertainers — though so few of us actually know it.

As consumers, isn't this what we're looking for? Just like a movie trailer that oversells the film, how many times have you been duped by some slimy salesperson who overpromised and under-delivered? Some people will lie for their own selfishness, and it's unfortunate, as this creates a stigma that continues to plague the service industry and creates a lack of initial trust. And it's why when someone finds a great service provider, they shout their name from the rooftops!

What is relational selling?

Relational selling means being a relatable human and a professional at the same time. Consumers want a professional, but what they really want is someone they can talk to at their level about both business and personal things. For example, I can provide a reference by showing you my reviews. I can do this by visiting www.reviewsteve.com, or calling any current or past client (with their permission, of course), and putting them on the phone with my new prospect. My dad was big on having some of his past clients there for him if he needed to make a reference call to have the prospective customer feel better about going ahead with the work. A satisfied past client can make all the difference when building a relationship of trust. That handles professional credibility. But I can also bridge the *personal* gap by having a conversation about just about anything, allowing the conversation to flow away from business. Getting to know someone more personally develops a different kind of bond outside of the traditional professional-and-client dynamic.

Relational selling is so important when painting a picture, because authenticity is key to a good story. Loosen up when you're with people — you really are allowed to be yourself, as people relate to authentic versus "forced" selling.

Speaking of authentic and relatable, if you look at five of the most successful films and study why they connect at such a deep level with the general public, you can get an idea of what captures us as an audience. Consider the highly-acclaimed *The Godfather*, where Marlon Brando and Al Pacino create a masterful performance about family, the mob, violence and an emergence of Pacino as the good boy that takes over the family business and plots revenge. Then there's *The Shawshank Redemption*, where the characters played by Tim Robbins and Morgan Freeman develop a deep-rooted friendship behind bars after Robbins' character is wrongfully imprisoned for a crime that he didn't commit. Living under the tyranny of the warden and head guard, Robbins finds freedom and personal justice against his oppressors. *Pulp Fiction*, Quentin Tarantino's masterpiece, is a unique blend of storytelling mingled with amazing acting that references several story threads that eventually meet — and all hell breaks loose. Through the *Star Wars* franchise, George Lucas created another universe for us, leading us on a hero's journey through the light and dark side of the Force. In *Forest Gump*, Tom Hanks plays a simple character who loves easily, even though the woman he loves doesn't love him back the same way. He gave his all in everything he did, and fortune always found him, yet he was never looking for fortune itself.

Each of these films painted vivid pictures of people, places, and plots — but, more importantly, they made us *feel* something. They connect with us by tapping into the core aspects of our lives: truth, justice, fairness, ruthlessness, being an underdog, purity, and so on.

Music can do the same thing. Sometimes music connects us to the story being told on the screen, and sometimes it tells its own story, independent of a visual medium. Music seems almost magical in the way it can mesmerize us, make us move our bodies, and recall long-lost memories and emotions. Remember, painting a picture for your client doesn't always mean it has to be a mental image — it can be an emotional connection, and music does this effectively for so many people — even instrumental music (or music sung in a foreign language) can do the trick, drawing on the deepest parts of the listener's heart to bring about a change in perspective.

Can you see the power of layering through emotional connection now? Painting a picture is about tapping into what your prospective client holds dear through discovery, emotional connection, and humanizing the experience. Am I saying you should go to the movies with a prospect, or serenade them? Of course not — I'm showing you how storytelling — in whatever form — can truly help us connect with others in lasting and substantial, memorable ways.

One major benefit to this type of connection is you don't have to be the least expensive service to get the job, since happiness and dreams aren't something people want to put a price on. If you can paint a picture well enough and make that human connection, cost becomes secondary.

- So, what are *you* doing to paint people a picture when you're offering your service?
- What are you discovering about your prospect so you can connect at a deeper level?
- Are you painting value and professionalism?
- Are you painting experience and security?
- Are you painting vulnerability and openness, to build trust?

We are always interpreting the information that we receive, so put yourself in the prospect's shoes, and ask yourself how you would feel after an initial meeting with *you*. Would you ever want to hear from *you* again? Was there mild interest, but most likely forgettable in a short period of time? Are you eager to get started because the meeting surpassed your expectations?

We need to measure our own abilities in order to grow and better ourselves, so we can actually achieve what we set out to do, since most companies provide a baseline of sales expectations.

Δ Δ Δ

Let's recap the vital discoveries from Chapter 2 so you can improve your connecting abilities:

•   To "paint a picture" is to explain a process that connects your professional approach to an emotional state that your prospective client can relate to, all while humanizing the experience.

•   Consider all the channels of content out there that we gravitate toward, and how some ads make us cry, and others we don't even notice. What gets you connected to specific material versus all of the material we're bombarded with each day?

•   Which song is your favorite, and why? Which movie is your favorite, and why? Which book is your favorite and why? Don't stop at the first "why" answer you give yourself when answering these questions, dig several layers deeper to get at the heart of it, and you may be surprised with what you come up with.

• Video yourself with your phone talking to a mirror as if you were speaking to a prospect. See how natural you look while changing the emotional expressions on your face and in the tone of your voice. Try a variety of emotions: excited, caring, upset, protective. There's no better way to become your best without knowing how the outside world sees you. Unless you spend a lot of time reviewing videos of yourself, you likely have no idea how the outside world sees you.

CHAPTER 3

YOUR QUALIFYING ACRONYM

Remember the four types of people my father would meet when door-knocking? How did he know which was which? *Qualifying*.

In the world of real estate, I learned long ago that through qualifying, I get to understand what my prospect's wants, needs and musts are — and whether or not they're a good fit for what I'm selling.

The word *sell* comes from the Old English word *sellan*, which means "to give."[6] Instead of thinking of selling in the traditional sense (*getting* a sale); think of it in terms of giving: give understanding, provide connection, offer value. Coming from a place of giving builds trust as you work through your qualifying process. When you qualify a prospect, you're giving them a chance to determine if they're the right person for your offering!

While everyone is a potential client, not everyone is an ideal client.

While each person you meet is someone who *may* become a client, only the ones you *qualify* are truly a potential client. Some people are simply not a fit. The only way to tell is to find out their wants, needs, and musts. Together, as you move along an uncharted roadmap and through discussion, you have an opportunity to discover, validate and/or alter their plans based on the answers you get to a very specific set of qualifying questions.

Remember, the job of the professional is to make sense of what the prospect wants, and then explain and connect to how it's achievable or unrealistic. If unrealistic, make sure you put a plan together to help them see a new vision, and don't make them feel poorly about having to adjust what they're connected to.

Qualifying is a guidance system, and if you're off target, even by the slightest of margins, all parties will miss the intended target. Think of a rocket's guidance system: even if a vessel flying from the earth to the moon is 99 percent accurate in its trajectory, the 1 percent miscalculation will cause it to miss the moon by 4,169 miles.

There's no difference in qualifying a prospect.

If you don't follow a process that checks off the necessary boxes, the likelihood of hitting your intended target will be low. In science, such calculation mistakes ensure failure. In the service industry, you may have a chance at getting lucky, but what busy professional has time for luck? You may not be a busy professional yet, but why wait on implementing a framework to your success? Putting effective systems in place now can help you reach that success level even sooner!

Acronyms act as our guidance system

I created this acronym for car dealers to use, so they can better understand if a prospect wants to move forward with a purchase or not in a minimal amount of time, and it covers all the bases:

M (model)
E (extras/features)
NU (new or used)
P (price)
F (financing)
T (trade in)
C (competition)
M (motivation or timing)
D (test drive)
= MENU-PFTC-MD

Using an acronym provides a framework for each interaction, so you never lose your place in a qualifying conversation.

As you begin to incorporate a qualifying acronym into your day-to-day conversations, and work to find out what your prospect is after, you'll notice a few major changes in your business practice. Using a strong acronym can increase the likelihood of having prospects jump ship and decide to work with you over a competitor they're currently talking to because you were more detailed and focused. You'll never feel lost again in a conversation, as you'll have a grip on what you'll need to accomplish conversationally in order to qualify the prospect thoroughly. You can develop an acronym for pretty much anything, as you'll notice that most qualifying questions, regardless of industry, are fairly similar. This is because qualifying always centers around understanding the decision-maker's concerns about money, timing, wants, needs, and attitude toward current competition.

Having such a structure gives you confidence in yourself, and builds others' confidence in you, which is critical to a smooth sales experience and to getting referrals in the future. When we feel a service provider is the complete package, and they've provided us with "above and beyond" service, we cherish them and refer them to as many people as we can. This is because great service combined with a great human is unfortunately more of a rarity than commonplace in this world — so we feel compelled to share. Just the way we like to share a great movie or piece of music — we're personally connected, and want others to feel that same connection.

Sadly, many service providers don't

provide much structure or guidance regarding what's about to take place as the sales process moves forward. The uncertainty that instills in a prospect can derail a potential deal, as they lose confidence in you. Think of yourself as the consumer for a moment: would you feel excited and optimistic after hearing your own pitch? As long as you're being honest with yourself, that answer will tell you a lot about how to improve your process.

So, here's the qualifying acronym I use in real estate (you can always create an acronym that's more specific to your industry):

LPMAMA

Each letter stands for a critical piece of information you'll need to fully understand so you can help your prospective client piece their real estate puzzle together with you. It all begins with understanding where they want to live.

L = Location
The very first thing I'll need to know from my prospect is where they want to live. Once they answer, I always ask if there are any secondary areas they're also interested in. The last thing we want to do is focus on one part of the city if the prospect is interested in a few areas. Most people don't just volunteer information, so if you don't ask the secondary

question, it's possible that inventory is low in their number one area and it takes time to find them the right home. In the meantime, they're getting frustrated with the waiting process and immediately begin to look online to see what else is out there, and since you weren't sending them this information, their loyalty to you can be cut like a piece of string. When that happens, a home may pop up in their desired area, and when you follow up to schedule a viewing, you find out they bought a home through another agent in that other part of town. Some agents like to say, "buyers are liars," but I don't believe that. I believe if we do our jobs correctly and dig deep, people will tell you everything, and they will be loyal — but only if you give them a reason to be, by listening and responding appropriately and in a timely manner.

P = Price

Everybody has a price point they feel comfortable with. Even if they can afford more, people have a general idea of what they want to spend on a home. You want to establish this, so you can create a range in their search parameters when setting up a search for them.

M = Mortgage

I always ask if they will be paying cash or financing the property purchase. Here in San Diego, there are so many cash buyers — and I'm not talking $300,000, I'm talking up into the multi millions — so never be afraid to ask if cash is an option for people. On the financing side (the most common way to buy), I need to understand where they are in this process, since the sale can't happen without a financial exchange. I need to know if they've spoken with a lender yet, who the lender is, and where they are with their pre-approval. Once I understand this, I can lead them to a preferred lender I know will take absolute care of them and find out from the expert where the prospect stands financially, and can we get the green light to begin viewing homes. Without the money in place, why would you take someone out to view property? If they don't know if they're financially ready, or if their price point doesn't jive with reality, better to find out in the beginning instead of days or weeks later when you write an offer. You need to be very careful in this process, because some of the people you begin working with will want to get out and view as many homes as possible because they're excited — but what does that do to your time? It's absolutely critical to ensure the money is a non-issue and that the price range is firmly established, so the prospect can feel comfortable proceeding.

A = Agent

I always ask prospects if there's a professional like me already helping them with their real estate needs. You really don't want to be helping someone for a period of time, only to discover they felt bad letting you know there was already someone helping them. As much as you want to blame the prospect, it's always the service provider's responsibility to ask these questions. Again, this is where the "buyers are liars" comes in, and honestly, these questions are on you. Nobody wants to be in this situation...so *ask!*

M = Motivation

Timing is everything in a transaction, and without knowing what the prospect's timing is, you could be spinning your wheels for quite some time. Just because a prospect has extreme excitement about the process and they can't wait to find their new home, or whatever it may be that you're helping them with, if their timeline isn't for 8-12 months, there isn't any real urgency to begin showing them homes today. You'll always need to know (in a real estate setting) if they currently own a home or if they're renting. If owning, do they wish to keep the home and rent it out? Or do they need to sell it? If they're renting, are they locked into a lease for some time, or are they month-to-month? You need to know how motivated the buyer is to move, so you know where to focus your efforts and with what level of urgency.

A = Appointment

This is where you take all of the information the prospect provided you and decide on what the appointment looks like, and how to build a plan around the prospect's future needs. I've found this process to be a game changer for me, as it's allowed me to understand exactly what was going on with each prospect I spoke with. To get a real 360-degree view of the situation, you need to ask the right questions (above), and make sure you note all their answers. Good decisions are based on good data. You need all the right information to help your prospect make the right decisions. Partial answers or missing answers will not be enough. Better to get the answers you need — and not hesitate to go layers deep — as the true reasons are needed, not superficial responses. Please understand that you are the *leader* of this process, not the other way around. If the prospect was the professional, what would they need *you* for? I can assure you that your conversations will go exponentially better now that you have a framework to follow, so that the appointments you set will have real potential to close.

Now, if you're not in the real estate industry, don't worry — there will be many similarities to the fundamental principles in this

LPMAMA acronym that still apply to you and your industry. Just ask yourself what it is that you need to know for appropriately helping your prospect — what are the "must-have" pieces of data — so you can get the answers you need and proceed confidently. As I mentioned, the components of the qualifying acronym are all geared at cutting to the heart of the most relevant questions: money, timing, decision makers, competition, wants, needs, and so on. You know exactly what information you'll need in order to design your acronym accordingly.

Once you have your qualifying acronym, follow it like a pilot follows their pre-flight checklist before takeoff. A pilot doesn't just push a button and the engines roar to life. Quite the opposite; they go through a specific, ordered list each and every time to ensure a safe flight and that everything is in working order before they put themselves and their passengers in a position they can't come back from. Make your list. Practice your list. Follow it to a tee every time, so you can navigate the conversation to the desired conclusion: a deal, no deal, or no deal at this time.

Role Playing as a Way of Life

I just mentioned practice, and let me tell you, as soon as I saw and felt the benefit of bringing clarity and structure to my work life, I wasn't just hungry to keep improving, I was starving for more. The real breakthrough for me came when our real estate office began implementing recorded role play calls.

On Mondays, Wednesdays, and Fridays we went over buyer scenarios. On Tuesdays and Thursdays, we went over seller scenarios. My broker at the time would chuckle at me because I would say that "role play changed my life." But I'm serious: I never would have even written this book if not for the power of role play, nor would I have engaged in as many speaking and teaching opportunities as I do. It's all about the role play!

Setting up regular role-playing opportunities is easier than you may think. Our office created a Monday-through-Friday role-play scenario intended for use each morning. We'd call into the recorded line as part of our daily routine. If you're interested in such a program, and your office doesn't already have a role-play program set up, you can run it by your management and be the one to get the ball rolling. What business wouldn't want to be proactive in elevating the customer experience through role play? And if you want to take it to a whole other level, you can create your own meet-up and invite various professionals to join, as a way to build your network while polishing your pitch.

Part of my own business plan for coaching includes recording professional speaker clients as they present. We use the recording to make improvements, just like a like a golf swing simulator is used for breaking down what's working and establishing places the golfer can make adjustments and hit the ball further and more consistently. The focus is on presentation style, voice, tonality, word use, and physiology. Make this part of your plan, and watch your skills soar.

I think I can hear you saying, "Come on, Steven, seriously? Role playing?" Look, I'm not going to say it was easy for me to accept the idea at first, either. The thought of being on a call with my peers was daunting: would there be judgement? How vulnerable would I allow myself to be? Maybe I wouldn't sound as smart as I thought I was. So much gets said in our own minds when we step out into the unknown, yet nothing killed me or stabbed me in the back as I kept improving. Yes, I survived. And I quickly grew to love it — because I saw the results. Role play wasn't the scary thing I thought it would be — there were just good solid people on these calls looking to improve, and learn new techniques. The participants were invaluable because of their feedback, which ultimately helped me improve my qualifying skills. Without them, I would have no idea where I stood in my development, and without that, how could I continue to get any better?

Initially, an overwhelming amount of role

play participants say it's harder to feel natural in one of our calls than if they were speaking with a prospective client. That type of statement is all about ego getting in the way, since it's not every day that we're performing before our peers. We default to feeling uncomfortable when the process is unknown to us, and it takes time to make role play our new normal, but isn't that how it is in everything we do? If you work out legs for the first time in months being away from the gym, no matter what shape your legs were in, the next few recovery days are going to be murder. But once you begin working out your legs on a regular basis, you're not afraid of the next leg day — you just do it. That's how it is with role play — no one on the other end of the line is going to jump through the phone and bite you for saying something that may not be ideal in the role play conversation. They'll make a note and gently point it out at the end of your call. Embrace the growth, even if your role play muscle has never been worked out before, because when it gets strong, you're going to kick some ass and feel unstoppable when you talk to anyone — not just a prospect.

I cannot overemphasize the value of role playing. Once engaged in these critical practice sessions, I became obsessed with mastering the art of the conversation. Role play was so good for me, and the feedback was exactly what I needed to help me get to the next level — so much improvement took place in how I spoke on an everyday level. I learned to change up my cadence, tone, and pitch at will, and the benefit of this improvement is that it crossed over into my personal life and helped me connect deeper with those closest to me.

Now, I've spoken quite a bit about role playing here in this chapter that's about the qualifying acronym. I'm sure you've put the two together. The best way to perfect the systemized use of your qualifying acronym is through (say it with me!) ROLE PLAYING. Get curious about having a qualifying acronym that you can use over and over in your business. Practice that acronym with role playing. Rinse, and repeat.

Business isn't a life or death situation, but if you're taking care of a family financially, if you're missing an important event that is dear to you, if you're reducing quality time with friends, or whatever else you can remind yourself of when you're reading this paragraph, ask yourself why you're disrespecting yourself and those around you by not asking the tough questions. Once you begin to employ your qualifying acronym, I'm not saying your success will be 100 percent, as sometimes situations change. But what I am saying is you will be able to more quickly distinguish reality from fiction, and at a much higher percentage of success, once you employ the qualifying acronym framework.

△ △ △

Let's recap the vital discoveries from Chapter 3 so you can improve your qualifying abilities:

•   Qualifying acts as a guidance system, and if it isn't followed properly, all parties will likely miss the intended target

•   Ask yourself if you're working with any current structure when it comes to qualifying, and how effective it is

•   A qualifying acronym is made up of specifically designed letters, each representing a subject critical to understanding the prospect's needs, wants, and musts

•   The acronym is the framework you'll work within for each and every qualifying conversation you'll have

•   The best way to become proficient in the systematized use of your qualifying acronym is through role playing

CHAPTER 4

FIRST IMPRESSIONS, MIRRORING, AND MATCHING

There used to be an old TV ad for shampoo with the tag line, "You never get a second chance to make a first impression." Cheesy as the ad may be, the principle is true. Humans naturally make snap judgments when they meet other humans — often subconsciously. And when I say "snap," I mean SNAP. Judgments can literally take place in *one tenth of a second*.[7]

Where do those judgments come from, and how are they formed? Since information is power, the more we understand about how we operate as individuals, the easier it becomes to think outside of ourselves and shift perspective to, "How does someone see us when we show up?" How does this factor into our business model, and how does it affect how we connect with others?

Studies show that mimicking the body language and gestures of a person you're communicating with (mirroring and matching) can make that person feel more engaged and open towards you. As we dive into this segment, I want to touch on the process behind how we operate during first contact, and how we eventually get into a rapport. Judgment and perspective happen whether you like it or not, regardless of who you are. To avoid incorrect judgments — or prejudgments based on that first impression — make sure:

- You're dressed appropriately
- You've showered and taken care of any particular odors that can turn off a prospect
- You have a firm, yet respectful handshake
- You smile and have the appearance of being pleasant
- You're courteous and use "please" and "thank you"
- You don't interrupt people when they're talking
- You're engaging
- You avoid pulling up to meet your client in a car that looks beat up or that was in an accident

Appearances Matter

There was once a new pastor assigned to lead a large church. Since none of the congregants had met the new pastor, he conducted an experiment. He dressed up as a homeless person the day he was to be introduced to the congregation. Showing up early as people were flowing into church, he asked the members for money to buy food. No one gave him a penny. He then went to the front of the church and took a seat, and was quickly asked to move to the back. He continued greeting people from the back of the church as they arrived, and received several dirty looks. It was time for church to begin, and the elders, who were in on this ruse, began to read the announcements. When it was time to introduce the new pastor, the congregation gave a thunderous applause in excited anticipation...but then the "homeless man" stood up and made his way to the front. He walked up to the altar, took the microphone and began to recite a verse from the Bible. Once he was done reciting the verse, he let the congregation know what he had experienced that morning, and many people in the congregation wept or had their heads lowered in shame. The pastor let the congregation out early that day so they could go home and reflect on what had just happened.

This story may seem extreme, but since we all judge what we see before us, never assume that what we see matches the story we've created for ourselves.

As a service provider, you don't want to knock yourself out of contention because you're not taking care of the exterior, as this is something you have control over. Furthermore, the story about the pastor would likely happen again and again in repeated random churches if the scenario was played out the same way. I'm not supporting the actions of the congregants, but this is the way our brains our wired — we simply tend to naturally judge based on what we can see, hear, smell, touch and taste. Ask yourself how *you* would react if a homeless person was in your place of worship asking you for food or money? Even though there was a deeper lesson for the congregation to absorb, that doesn't mean we won't repeat our actions the same way in the future if we find ourselves in an uncomfortable situation.

Early on in my career, I went to an expired listing appointment (the home hadn't sold, and I wanted to be the seller's new agent). I visited them at their home to provide my opinion of the home's value, and to discuss becoming their listing agent. I drove up to the home and parked out front in my white Volkswagen Jetta. Unbeknownst to me, the sellers were focused on the kind of car I drove. As we got to talking, they grew to like me, and told me that they'd have likely turned me away if I had been driving some fancy luxury car.

Think about that for a moment: before I ever had a chance to meet the sellers or make a personal impression, I was being judged based on the car I drove — before I ever set foot in their home! They had a perception that a luxury car meant a slick salesman, and they weren't going to be victims of someone's expensive taste. Now, of course, that's just one person's perception and opinion — whether you have a nice car or not has no real bearing on your integrity or your ability to be a good service provider — but it mattered to these people for whatever reason. In the end, I passed their judgment test and got the listing — and sold their home.

My father also believed in a very conservative approach. He wore jeans and a blazer every day to work, and preferred to look unassuming instead of flashy. He drove your everyday Chevy and never wanted a prospect to think about how much money he was making in the transaction, based on the clothes he wore or the car he drove.

How Do Appearances and First Impressions Impact Your Interactions?

When you see someone enjoying luxury products, what do you think? If someone drives by in a Lamborghini, Ferrari, or Rolls Royce, do you judge them somehow? What thoughts pop up when someone you're talking to is wearing a gold Rolex? We all mentally slap labels onto everything based on what we see, often subconsciously.

When we do that, we start to create our own interpretations of who and what the person is:

- Strong
- Nice
- Safe
- Rich
- Poor
- Talker

- Too good for you
- Friendly
- Dangerous
- Deserving
- Elite
- Thief

Knowing how important first impressions are, and realizing that we judge *and are judged* in a tenth of a second…what do you do next? **You learn to mirror and match.** This means you *adjust* and *synchronize* how you communicate verbally and through the use of body language. Once you're trained in this ability, you'll be able to easily connect to your prospects' frequency and communicate on their level and at their pace.

Let's focus on:

- Tone of voice
- Rate of speech
- Finishing sentences with an upward inflection (as if asking a question) or a downward inflection (making a point or a statement)

- Body language (hunched over, sitting straight and stiff, animated…)
- Facial expressions (some people are animated, serious, sad, weary, expressionless…)

According to an article in *Wired Magazine* about the science of meeting people, how strong and competent someone is makes up about 80 to 90% of the overall first impression, *and that holds true across all cultures.*[8]

Attractiveness, likeability, competence, trustworthiness, and aggressiveness were measured in a study by Willis and Todorov.[9] They asked university students to look at photos for 100 milliseconds and determine what trait stood out for them. Trustworthiness was the consistent trait that stood out as the highest factor for the students.

The Communication X-Factor

The "x-factor" in our human interactions is *discerning and understanding personality type.* This really is like putting a puzzle together. Everyone is constantly building that puzzle for each person they encounter. We can't help but make judgments on everything we decide to do, yet we somehow forget that we're also being judged in that same way by others. You need to understand that you're being judged for personality type *from the moment* someone sees you, or hears you on the phone. So, you need to present yourself in the best possible light *right from the beginning*, and *direct* others past that "pre-judgement" phase.

On the opposite side of that perception bridge is your own understanding of the other person. To understand how to take on the prospect's communication style, so you can get into a rapport and move through the vetting process to earn their business, you need to quickly make an accurate assessment of their personality type.

Have you ever taken a personality test? They can be revealing and shocking, prompting you to perhaps question the methodology, if the results fail to align with your self-perceptions. We all think we're a perfectly unique individual — and we are — but we're also all humans, and therefore share certain traits. There are several testing instruments available that can describe us quite accurately, and it can be a bit mind-boggling when reading the final report.

The most critical component to mastering mirroring and matching is understanding personality type. Assessments such as Myers Briggs, BANK or DISC may vary somewhat on the surface level and terminology used, but all you really need to know is what type of personality you're dealing with. I recently took a test at www.16personalities.com, and it quite accurately replicated the Myers Briggs test results: ENFJ-A. This means I'm ridiculously extroverted, and my preferred role is diplomat, with my strategy being people mastery. The test labeled me as a Protagonist, and indicated that I'm a natural-born leader, full of passion and charisma. Forming around two percent of the population, Protagonists are oftentimes politicians, coaches, and teachers, reaching out and inspiring others to achieve and to do good in the world. With a natural confidence that begets influence, Protagonists take a great deal of pride and joy in guiding others to work together to improve themselves and their community.[10] This truly is me! And let me tell you how odd it feels to have some test describe me! But it works, and you can become as adept at these tests and this kind of simple profiling.

How to Mirror and Match

When you begin a conversation and you start your mirroring and matching, you must be mindful of how to connect with people on their level, and employ these essential skills:

• *Mimic their physiology* — If they're expressive, be expressive (or more than you usually are if you typically don't show much expression). If they smile often, smile often. If they fold their arms, fold your arms a few seconds later. Eventually, when you get into a rapport, you can lean forward and they will lean forward. This is when you know you've achieved a rapport.

• *Watch your rate of speech* — There's nothing that seems more "off" when speaking with someone than listening to a fast-talking city-slicker or a slow-talking rural person. It's important to maintain a natural speaking rate to keep your listener engaged and interested. Too fast, and you can lose them or make them feel anxious. Too slow, and you'll bore them to death or lose their attention. Just right, and you can have engaging conversation. Be mindful of this, as being out of balance in this area can cause your connection to fade quickly.

• *Manage your decibel level* — You really want to make sure you can be heard, so don't be afraid to speak up. But, if your client speaks in a whisper and leans in, then you'd better whisper and lean in. This will create a bond quickly. If your prospect is a loud talker and you speak loud in turn, they'll warm up to you super quickly, since most people don't talk very loudly.

• *Consider tonality and pitch* — Make sure you pay attention to the emotion your interlocutor is expressing during your conversation, as that emotional connection will tap into their feelings, and that's where true connection happens. The whole goal is to connect on that emotional level. So, if the pitch of the prospect's voice goes up during certain words, you do the same. Anytime someone feels like they're talking to someone like them, it goes a long way in establishing trust early on in a conversation.

Now think about the following four critical conversational desires as you apply the above skills. If you want your prospect to feel comfortable with you as their service provider, these four considerations must become part of your dialogue toolbox:

1.   **We all want to be heard.** No one wants to be talking to someone who isn't paying attention, right? Have you ever been there? I've not only been there, but I've been the one doing it to people in the past. Now, more than ever, it's a common occurrence as we give our phones more attention than the person in front of us — it even has a name: *phubbing* (a portmanteau of "phone" and "snubbing"). Being heard is satisfying.

2.   **We all want to be acknowledged.** Look at the person who's talking to you, and nod your head "yes" and have facial expressions that match your emotion. Happy, smile. Sad, frown. You get the drill, have your physiology show up and contribute to your responses. It goes a long way!

3.   **We all want to be understood.**

Understanding is demonstrated when you can repeat back to the prospect the meaningful information you just heard from them, so they know you understand their needs and they can confirm that you're on the right track — or they add in something you missed, or that they thought of, to add to what's important to them. This is a key element of what's called *active listening.*

4. **We all want to be taken care of.** Once your prospect feels like they've been heard, acknowledged, and understood, and you've given them professional knowledge and/or solutions demonstrating how *your* service will address their issues and ease their specific pain points, the prospect will feel a sense of relief and begin to trust that you're the right service provider for them.

Listening is the Key

In case you weren't listening... LISTENING IS THE KEY. In other words, the first basic step to learning this part of your craft is to start paying attention to how people talk. Do they speak slowly? Quickly? Do they pause in thought before they speak? Just pay attention and have fun experimenting with talking more like the person in front of you. Pay attention to their hand motions and other body gestures. See how expressive their faces are, and play with that.

Now, you might be thinking, "But that's not me! I can't do that!" I disagree. You can do anything, if you just get out of your own way mentally, and simply allow yourself to *get uncomfortable* with who you are, so you can achieve *who you wish to become*. If you think about it, who are you really? You're a set of learned experiences, and you act out and live your life according to your beliefs. The people you meet are no different, and that's why it's important to learn how to connect based on the principles of this chapter.

Learn to enjoy playing with the skills and tools above. If you do, you'll quickly notice how people express themselves. You'll watch people nod their head "yes" as you're speaking when they buy into your message. As you get more and more comfortable with this process, and begin to implement it into your personal and professional life, please act responsibly, as you'll be on your way to becoming an *influencer*.

Δ Δ Δ

Here are a few simple exercises you can do to get a feel for this new skill set:

•   The next person you meet who talks quickly: pick up your pace

•   The next person who speaks with their hands: begin to move your hands when it's your turn to speak. Just use subtle gestures, so you don't look like a conductor at a symphony or like you're mocking them.

•   Next time you're talking to someone when you're both sitting down and they lean in: lean in yourself, and then after a minute or so of good conversation, lean back. Observe if they lean back after you do.

•   When you're really in a great conversation with someone: wipe the tip of your nose and see if they do too a few seconds later. With this one, you'll need to be face to face, relatively close, and in great conversation. *Warning: when it works for the first time, you might just laugh out loud!*

CHAPTER 5

WORD POLISH

Language is leverage. I don't believe many of us realize just how important and powerful language is, and the role it plays in our lives every day. Most of us speak to communicate something without realizing there may be a better way to structure a sentence, or that we can work with our words as if they were pieces in a chess match.

Pause for a moment and visualize what I'm about to say, so you can better understand why I'm saying that language is leverage. If you see someone who's visually upset and crying, you can go over and comfort them with a hug — you know, one of those hugs where you lean in, rub their back and hold them, providing a sense of security. Now, if you add *language* to the hug, while rubbing their back and saying in a sad whisper, "I'm so sorry, I really am so sorry," and you empathize with whatever they're going through, you're leveraging words to communicate how you feel and achieving a connection at a deeper level.

Words can be used to make peace, and they can be used to bring on destruction. Remember the power of words, because only *you* control what comes out of your mouth. I believe words should be used to inquire, connect and accomplish. Words help me discover all that I need to know in order to serve my clients properly and effectively, and by blending mirroring and matching techniques, and then adding tonality and inflection on top of those words, I'm hitting home at a much deeper level as I work to connect. Just like there are only eight whole notes in music, that can be used an infinite number of ways, language may be bound by a finite vocabulary, but how you *use* those words is what really makes the difference in connecting with people.

I had a dream where I was speaking to a room full of people, and I was lecturing on what qualifying meant to me. It was an interesting dream, because it helped me connect even further with why I work so hard to connect and understand what my client's needs are, so that I can best serve them. I used to see qualifying through my acronym as a way to understand if my prospect was truly looking to buy or sell a home, instead of using the acronym as a way to fully connect and have them truly engage with me.

What I mean by fully connecting is

understanding at the deepest level what buying or selling a home *means* to them. When you can get to the emotional connection, not just the logic of why it makes sense to buy or sell, then you can humanize the experience. To *humanize* means to get to where we're talking like friends, and as we're chatting openly, we're really enjoying each other's company and we get into a much deeper level of conversation than just talking about real estate. Think about that: how often does that happen in a selling experience?

Once you fully grasp the weight of what this process means to your prospect and embody that as their advocate, you can work at a much deeper level for them, which means you'll fight for them and share their story if it's applicable to making the transaction work. I opened up this chapter with the word leverage. I used that word because it's not just a matter of leveraging yourself with your client — it's about taking the connection you've earned and leveraging your client's story to connect with the agent and their client on the other side of the transaction. I can't tell you how many transactions I've been involved in where the emotional connection I shared with the other side made them feel like my clients should be the ones to own the home that we submitted an offer on — and they too fought for us.

Words are what allow you to find your way into connection.

What I often find in my workplace are words or phrases that don't give the scenario a chance, like "waste of time." I absolutely love and despise hearing this phrase — for different reasons, of course. I love it when I hear a prospect say it because I reply with, "there is no such thing as a waste of time in my vocabulary." I let them know that whatever they may have believed was an insurmountable barrier may only be a temporary setback, and that I'll work tirelessly to help them remedy their issue.

What impact do you think that will have on the prospect? One of the reasons I despise "waste of time" is because we use it to defeat ourselves before we've even given the process a chance. When I take a different approach and show the prospect I'm going to help them accomplish their goal — regardless of the time and effort it takes — now the prospect feels like they have a champion for their cause — someone who cares and has a can-do attitude that perhaps makes up for their own uncertainty. I know that when I find myself on the receiving end of such a situation, I feel a sense of relief and gratitude that someone is there to truly help me — and that's the kind of trust I want to build with my prospects.

Turning someone's negative into a positive is like turning a frown upside down to get that smile. This is what happens when you help empower people and they feel this "wow" they may not have been expecting. When you can give people hope — something to shoot for — they will become a walking billboard advertising your services to others, because so few of us connect at such deep levels and demonstrate service that's designed around accomplishing your client's needs.

Language and words can *connect* and *empower*. Here are a few empowering words and phrases you may wish to incorporate into your vocabulary:

- We
- Share
- Together
- Take care of
- Find a way
- Put a plan together
- Look after
- Empower
- Collaborate
- I'll do that for you
- Let me look into that further
- I'll find out and get right back to you
- We'll work together
- Is there anything else you…?
- I'm/we're so excited for you
- My pleasure
- Please
- Appreciate
- Give back
- I understand
- I'll do everything I can
- Customer oriented
- Precise
- Professional
- Practical
- Diplomatic
- Patient
- Consistent
- Cooperative
- Attentive

- Committed
- Unconventional
- Resourceful
- Optimistic
- Accomplished
- Tolerant
- Hard working

- Observant
- Dependable
- Engaged
- Enthusiastic
- Responsive
- Persuasive

Notice a theme? It's all about being there for your prospect on the journey, letting them know you'll take care of them until, together, you successfully find the ideal solution. Use language that's results-oriented and time-oriented, to set realistic expectations on how you're going to help your prospect achieve their desired outcome — even if the process might seem to conflict with your prospect's desires. As a professional, you're expected to be the voice of reason and reality, so be sure to use empowering language that's aligned with their desires and sympathetic to their needs, but designed to help you match their perceptions with a more realistic vision.

Words Carry Weight

I was once interviewed by John Kitchens of the National Association of Expert Advisors (NAEA), and to make a point, I asked him to share an experience he went through where he was blown away by the service he received.

John told me that he was looking to do his

first triathlon, but that he hadn't been on a bicycle for as long as he could remember. The person who was helping him spent over an hour and a half with him and made him feel incredible about the adventure he was about to embark on. The service provider hooked John up with a bike at a fantastic deal and ensured John had everything he needed to begin his training properly. Because this person empowered John and took fantastic care of him throughout the qualifying and solution process, I asked John a question for which I already knew the answer: had he already referred this person or company to others? With a big grin, John said he'd already referred this person three to four times. It turns out the person was the general manager of the bike shop, but had never mentioned it — he simply took care of John. The language he used was non-threatening, aligning, and comforting; in the sense that John could ease back and let someone take care of him, because of the trusting environment created. The service provider never pushed the sale or pressured John; he simply discovered what was important to John and found solutions at a hugely discounted price, and never worked to upsell needlessly.

That's the experience we're all looking for when we employ people to solve our problems. I use the word "problem" to mean any "pain point" that we want addressed. For example, being hungry is a problem that we solve by either going to a grocery store or a restaurant, so we can take care of the hunger issue. Economic transactions that we seek out are often for the purpose of remedying some kind of problem.

So, as you set out to help people solve their problems, be mindful that your words carry weight, meaning, feeling, and importance.

I believe language is underutilized — that we fail to make the most of its amazing abilities to connect and influence. This is especially true in an age where asynchronous communication (text, chat, and email) is prioritized. We're continually developing new forms of language through abbreviated words and the use of emojis, which have their own strengths and weaknesses in terms of forming connections through language. Now more than ever, it's critically important that we bring an understanding of communication back to the forefront, since so many exchanges have devolved into super-quick replies that lack deep thought and a personal touch. Gmail will even give you a selection of canned responses to emails. The robots are smart, but they can never replace a true human interaction, and definitely won't help you stand out over another service provider as the best choice. Such tools also can make us reliant on them, such that we don't even know what to say in person.

Want to know what to say in person?

Take some time to watch a few of the all-time great interviewers. Just hit YouTube and search Howard Stern, Barbara Walters, Mike Wallace, Larry King, Oprah Winfrey, Charlie Rose, and Thomas Bilyeu, to name a few. I remember watching Larry King, and observed how he would lean his chin into the palm of his hand, with his elbow anchored to the table for support, and he would just gaze at his guest and let them talk. He just looked on like a little kid fascinated with whatever answer came out of their mouth. What a great example of engaged listening!

When I say, "Go watch YouTube," I'm telling you that you won't learn everything you need just by reading this book and following my instructions. You're responsible for your own growth, and it's up to you to become immersed in learning and observant about what you're seeing in these interviewers and how they connect with people to draw out their message in a way that an audience can relate to. Look at the great examples, and overlay the principles in this chapter, then begin to apply those ideas in your own linguistic behaviors.

$$\Delta \, \Delta \, \Delta$$

Let's review how you can take the knowledge from Chapter 5 and apply it so you can improve your language abilities:

•   Look back at the list of connecting and empowering words. Ask yourself if you're already using these consistently. If not, begin implementing them into your daily conversations and observe the effects.

•   Layer the words you use with tonality so you can convey emotion in your language.

•   Use a recording device so you can listen to yourself and how you sound. Without a feedback mechanism and a true measure, change will be difficult to implement effectively.

•   Say the word "why" with three different meanings. You can say it as a question with an upswing (meaning it sounds like you're asking for an answer to something). Then say "why" with a downswing meaning your making a point, which is more of an angry type question.

Lastly say "why" with some laughter in the word as if you're pleasantly surprised, as someone did something nice for you and you're questioning it, yet happy about it. You see, you can use language this way all the time if you know how to emphasize a word, as that word will take on a meaning of its own based on proper inflectional usage.

• Another great drill is to say the following four-word sentences and note how word order and emphasis can alter the meaning, sometimes significantly:

    o Only *I* love you.
    o I only *love* you.
    o I *love* only you.
    o I love *you* only.

CHAPTER 6

FINDING OPPORTUNITY

For me, this is where the magic lives. Once you become proficient in your business acronym, mirroring and matching, and word polish, you can begin to see beneath the surface to *the story behind the story*.

We humans have a remarkable ability to detect physiological change in others — especially if you know what to look for and how to interpret your observations. We call it "body language" precisely because such non-verbal cues are a language all their own, conveying meaning that can have a huge impact if you're "fluent in the language." From breathing patterns to stances to eye movements and other "tells," knowing this language can make a real difference in your personal and professional life.

There was a television show that aired for three seasons a few years ago called *Lie to Me*, starring Tim Roth. The whole premise of the show was how a trained eye can focus on universal micro-expressions in order to discern truth. In the show, the protagonist consulted with law enforcement to solve crimes. In real life, if you pay close attention to these micro-expressions, they can give you insight into what your prospect is experiencing emotionally — perhaps even what they're thinking but not expressing verbally or intentionally — and that can help improve your connection and build a rapport.

The seven universal micro-expressions are:

1. Happiness
2. Sadness
3. Fear
4. Disgust
5. Anger
6. Contempt
7. Surprise

In the service industry, your job and mine is all about *observing* and *connecting*. As a critical listener, staying laser-focused on noticing and interpreting physiological changes in the body of the person you're speaking with can let you know if your own responses are on point. Or, perhaps the other person's physiology is indicating that they're telling you something that isn't quite true, or maybe not the full story required for properly providing your service. Paying attention to these cues can really make a difference, but you have to understand what they are.

The primary cues are facial expressions, eye movement, breathing patterns, and changes in the tone of voice. As you become adept at identifying these physiological indications, it will begin to become second nature, and you'll also find that you're better able to make yourself vulnerable and open on your end of the conversation, so you can humanize yourself and be more than just a professional. This goes a long way to establishing trust.

The Eyes Have It

The eyes are the most important "tell" when it comes to being in a rapport and building trust. They say "the eyes are the windows to the soul" for a reason — someone's eyes can really tell you a lot. The human face moves around the eyes, as a part of the natural creation of facial expression. All your eyes can do is move up, down, left and right, but your face expresses how you feel. The conscious avoidance of emotional display is the "poker face," employed by professional gamblers to prevent their opponents from gauging any feelings associated with their hidden hand of cards. While some people may try to put on a poker face, most will end up giving away a lot through the subtle movements around their eyes.

In everyday life, people generally have a desire to share their thoughts, dreams, and desires. But many times, their own personal reasons make them uncomfortable with simply opening up right from the start — often out of feelings of guilt or inadequacy. Getting people to open up is where your job gets interesting, since you have to find *opportunity* in the feelings you're detecting as you strive to connect. As you start to get through, you'll see faces relax, bodies unfold from closed positions and a natural conversation ensue.

Make sure you're making eye contact, as they're watching *you* as well. Don't think you're the only one reading body language — there's always something going on subconsciously with your prospect. If the prospect senses weakness or insecurity, they'll judge you based on that (consciously or otherwise), so make sure you're strong in your gaze and have a radiating warmth about you. That means: be pleasant, wear a smile, unfold your arms, loosen your muscles, and be detailed and professional when you have to. Express positive feelings, rather than being closed, cold, and only logic-based. Again, pay attention to the eyes — everything else follows from there.

Take a Breath

Studying breathing patterns can be fascinating and challenging, since you need to watch the body's rhythmic pattern, which can be more subtle than the expressions of the eyes. When all is well, the breathing won't be noticeable, a normalized, steady breath being the default. But if something changes in the prospect's emotional state, you might hear a sharp inhale or exhale. That alteration in breath is a sign that something happened in their mind, and even if their words are no indication, they're suddenly prepared to either attack or defend against something that was just said.

Be mindful of the various breathing cues. For example, a large exhalation can be a sign of discontent or frustration. If you see that happen, address it by pausing and digging into what just happened for your prospect. Ask the gentle probing questions that can help explain their physiological reaction. This is why "finding opportunity" is so amazing — if asked, people really will tell you when you're out of alignment, or that the rapport you've developed is in jeopardy of breaking.

It takes time to build rapport and trust, but it takes no time to destroy it.

This is why learning about how people react is so critical to your success. These skills won't come to you overnight; they'll depend heavily on the relentless learning and practicing of the first three steps in this book. Master those, and then you can make this magic happen! As you become more versed in recognizing micro expressions, the smallest tells will seem as evident as someone getting shocked with electricity. A tiny facial difference will be read loud and clear, and you'll understand how to adjust the conversation before you fall out of the rapport.

Wrangling That Rapport

"Yes" patterns are also important to pay attention to. This isn't just about getting your client to verbalize "yes" over and over again — it can be as simple as seeing the "yes" in their repeated head nods and other "yes"-oriented physiology. When a prospect is fully engaged with your approach, their gaze will be firmly fixed upon you, their eyes will be open wider, and they'll repeatedly nod their head in a "yes" fashion.

Another "tell" that indicates two people are getting excited in a conversation and finding alignment with one another is the cadence of speech. They'll start talking faster, accelerating like two race cars shooting around a track, and before you know it, the time has flown by. Establishing that kind of rapport is all part of the magic of connecting.

Case in point: I'm fortunate to be part of the most incredible networking company ever, called ProVisors. I have the pleasure of being connected to just over five hundred top professionals in San Diego who work in a wide variety of professions. I've become close with many in this organization; that closeness has created a relaxed atmosphere where you can just be yourself, with no need for false exteriors. There was a meeting I had with a trust attorney early on in my membership with ProVisors, at a point where I hadn't yet established my credibility with the group. There I was, just a real estate agent meeting with an uninterested trust attorney who seemed very closed and standoffish at first. His arms were crossed, legs were crossed, his body not facing me, and his gaze not engaged with me. So, I just jumped into getting to know him. As we spoke about who he was — where he came from and what brought him into his profession, and I shared the fact that I'm fascinated by communication — everything began to change. His arms uncrossed, his legs uncrossed, his body faced me, his eyes opened wider, and he was leaning on the table truly engaged with what we were talking about. I was acutely aware that he saw little to no value in me at the beginning of our meeting — because he didn't know me — but through letting that conversation unfold and applying mirroring and matching and all the other skills, we actually became friends. Now we look forward to seeing each other at group functions and occasionally go out for coffee or lunch. Thanks to establishing a rapport, I was able to be myself, connect, and build a relationship that I'm sure he didn't see coming.

And that's what you're looking for: developing a rapport and creating an alignment.

To do this effectively and consistently, you need to be mindful of the following four things and stick to the outline religiously. People want to be:

- Heard
- Acknowledged
- Understood
- Taken care of

You may recall that I talked a bit about these four essential principles in Chapter 4, but they're *so* important, I want to delve a little deeper into them here in Chapter 6. You'll need to focus on these four principles if you want to establish rapport and alignment through physiology. If you're perfectly on target with qualifying a prospect, you'll see that they're wide-eyed, facing you directly, nodding "yes" and clearly excited to get started. On the other hand, if you aren't paying attention to these four points, you may find yourself out of alignment: failing to nod in acknowledgement of what they're saying, not repeating what you've come to understand is important to them, and eventually failing to take care of them.

This is very simple, yet so many service people somehow fail to catch the vision and apply these four ideas in every interaction!

Being heard — Isn't that what we all want? When you're speaking to someone and they allow themselves to get distracted, how does it make you feel? Time for an honest self-assessment: are you listening to your prospect the same way you expect to be listened to? If you expect to be listened to, what feelings arise when your friends or family don't pay attention to you when you're speaking? Do you feel disrespected, frustrated — maybe even a little angry? As you can imagine, those are feelings you certainly don't want to inspire in your prospect. So, remember the golden rule and realize that you're no different from any prospect, were the roles to be reversed. Respect the importance of attentive listening.

Acknowledged — Since you're now listening intently to what your prospect has to say, make sure you demonstrate to them that you're listening by actually acknowledging them in a clear way. Don't just sit stone-faced, quiet, and rigid. Instead, nod your head "yes" if you agree with something. Smile and let your body language convey that you're an active part of the conversation. Also, make sure you provide your relevant professional point of view during the discussion, because that leads us into being understood.

Understood — When your prospect is really keying in and getting onboard because your qualifying acronym hit on all of their requirements (wants and needs), make sure you repeat the most important aspects back to them. When you're done going over the main topics, ask if there's anything else they wish to add, as people don't always remember everything on the first go around. If they say no, then you have the right framework to work from. If they add to it, now they've given you the complete package about what's important to them, and you're all on the same page. *It is critical to repeat back your understanding of what they've told you, because this confirms understanding and aligns expectations.*

Taken care of — This phase leads directly and naturally from being understood. When a prospect feels heard, acknowledged, and understood, they become *confident* in the fact that you will take care of them. I love this part of the process! By now, you've successfully laid the ground work through effective conversation — your prospect is solidly on their way to becoming a client because they've experienced your competency as a professional and enjoyed great dialogue to get to what's important to them. You've humanized yourself, so you don't come off as some sales commission robot, and created that magic of rapport. How can you not celebrate at this point? Not only have you undergone a transformation in your client's eyes, but hopefully the same thing has happened for you: they're no longer just a paycheck, they're a future walking billboard advertising your services on your behalf. They know you'll take care of them, and one day they'll take care of you, too!

Δ Δ Δ

Let's review how you can take the knowledge from Chapter 6 and apply it so you can truly find opportunity:

• Pay close attention how engaged your prospect is with you

• What is your prospect's body doing or telling you? Are they facing you, turned away from you, breaking eye contact often?

• What about your prospect's facial expression and gestures? Are their eyes wide open? Are they nodding their head in a "yes" fashion when you're speaking with them?

• If you notice your prospect's physiology telling a different story from what they're saying with they're words, stop and ask them what's going on. If you don't get to the root of what just happened, you'll likely lose them as a possible client.

•   Check out some videos on micro-expressions to notice the subtle changes in people's physiology, so you can recognize if something has changed in your prospect's alignment with you.

•   You'll move deeper into rapport building by ensuring your client is being *heard*, *acknowledged*, *understood* and *taken care of* by your professional communication approach. While going through this process, you'll notice any misalignment in connecting to their message and rapport building.

CHAPTER 7

REPUTATION

Reputation is the key to building clout and truly making a name for yourself. Think about it: why do some of the biggest sports labels in the world endorse athletes? Why does the name of the star player on a team sell exponentially more branded merchandise than any other player on the team?

Reputation!

There are two forms of reputation: one involves the "inner game" — the way we see ourselves — and the other is all about the "outer game" — the way the world sees us.

Internal Reputation

Our internal reputation is the most challenging, because it's constantly shaped by our self-talk — essentially, we are what we think. There's a documentary called *Notorious* that walks us through Connor McGreggor's life, from the time he was so poor he didn't have a pot to piss in, to when he earned the UFC championship in two weight classes. It's one of the best films I've ever seen that demonstrates what it takes to execute a personal vision and make it reality. It doesn't matter if you love McGreggor or hate him; he wanted to be number one in the world, and he did what it took to get there — with no short cuts. You can do that, too.

To begin your road to success, you must achieve the right mindset. Mindset is essential because of what I mentioned above about the two forms of reputation — the first one being internal. Your inner voice, that defines your reputation to yourself, is either building you up or tearing you down. There's a voice that screams at you to push harder and encourages you to move forward, and a voice that repeatedly gives you excuses to quit, or tells you that you aren't good enough or don't deserve it. You can choose which voice to heed.

I grew up a pretty good athlete, yet I hated long distance running. Whenever I would go for a run, my internal voice would look for reasons to make me stop. The voice would say that my breathing was too hard, or tell me to focus on the fact that my shins hurt, or produce some other ridiculous excuse — and I would listen to it and allow myself to walk for a while. I didn't really need to stop, but I allowed myself to give in to that voice. Sometimes that voice plays on the strong and misunderstood survival instinct, telling us that we must stop if we want to survive. It's actually a lie; if we want to survive and *thrive* we need to keep pushing through the hard things or things we don't enjoy!

Once I was running a business instead of a foot race, some of those same doubts and fears would creep in. I remember a time when I'd get an appointment where the home was in the seven figure price range, and I'd find a way to tell myself I didn't want to work with the people — that voice would tell me there must be something wrong with the wealthy clients that was not in alignment with how I saw myself, and that I therefore couldn't help them. Why would I say such things to myself? I didn't think I was good enough.

The first time I can remember truly challenging my internal reputation was when I went on a trek to Nepal to climb a mountain near Mt. Everest called Mt. Kalapathar. It was a thirteen-day journey that began in a town called Lukla, and I had no idea what I was about to embark on. I had done little to no preparation, including breaking in my new hiking boots, and thought how lovely it would be to get to see Everest, like it would be all roses and bubble gum. Looking back to when I was thirty-one, I realize how little I paid attention to training and planning!

I can't even begin to explain the scenery to you; unless you've been to the Himalayas, it's impossible to express how majestic they are —

how much larger than life they seem, and how small they make you feel. For me, those mountains made me realize I was just a speck enjoying their beauty. As we made our way ever closer to our final destination, some days were "altitude days," where we would break altitude barriers and then come back down to where we were camped. This was done so our body could build more red blood cells and have less chance of experiencing altitude sickness. I wasn't fairing very well, as my lovely small bladder syndrome wasn't on the same page with the constant hydration that was necessary to minimize the possibility of experiencing altitude sickness. So, I was peeing all the time and would constantly wake through the night so I wouldn't pee in my sleeping bag. We finally got to a position where we could summit Kalapathar, and it was going to be a long day. We had to get up at 4:00 a.m. and push to summit while we still had plenty of daylight to get back down and make it to our camp. That day was twelve or thirteen hours long.

I'm telling you this story because I always believed in myself deep down — I really thought that I could achieve great things — but rarely did I put that belief into practice. Yet here I was, stuck atop a mountain range, and mental toughness and fortitude were the only things I had to get me through to the finish. The only thing anyone could do for me was encourage me, but at this altitude, no one could help if something went wrong, and there wasn't enough oxygen for anyone to keep encouraging me. I finally got to experience the core of my own "never give up attitude," a part of me I had rarely explored. I told myself that I would sooner die than turn back, and I committed to summiting. My internal reputation skyrocketed, and I believed I was unstoppable. It was a defining moment, and I carry that experience to this day. When I got home, I started comparing summiting in Nepal to making calls, asking hard questions of prospects and being relentless when it came to follow-up. After that challenge, my professional difficulties seemed like nothing. And it's because that thirteen-day trek *changed how I spoke to myself*. The do-or-die conditions of that expedition taught me how to listen to the right voice, and not succumb to excuses.

That voice inside of you can take you all the way up or all the way down — it really is your decision, since what you say to yourself, and what you listen to, is a choice.

Here are some internal reputation questions you can ask yourself to take a good long look at who you are and how you show up:

• **How do you see yourself? Why?** This isn't a superficial question where you simply take the first answer you give yourself. Dig into that question, and attempt to go eight or nine layers deep into "how you see yourself." Then create a vision of who you know you are capable of being, and consciously work to see yourself that way from now on. Remember the lemon story earlier in this book: the lemon never existed, but your body began producing saliva as if the lemon were real. Imagine how that applies to internal reputation.

• **Who do you want to be? Are you there yet?** If not, what can you do *daily* to keep practicing and adjusting? It's vital to your achievement to have a mental routine that your internal reputation can benefit from. Marathon runners don't just show up and expect to run 26.2 miles without having first put in many hours of training. There's so much involved in the preparation — without putting in the work, you won't know how to overcome the obstacles you might encounter in the race. Be sure to track and measure your movement toward that transformation of internal reputation. You'll never know where you are in life if you don't keep a record of what you've done, and plan for where you're going.

• **What is your self-talk like?** You need to be aware and in control of who's talking internally, or you'll get the wrong messages when life gets challenging, when you're tired, or when you're just "over it." Practice making the voice of positive affirmation and good internal reputation the dominant voice in your mind — controlling the other voices like a coach telling his players what needs to be done to win the championship.

• **Are you embracing the journey?** The journey is about transformation, and transformation means change. Be prepared: you may outgrow friends and old habits that seemed great when you were stuck in your old patterns, but now are counterproductive to growing the "new you." You may find you're drawn to other crowds or new surroundings.

External Reputation

I once attended a Mike Ferry real estate seminar where he talked about "upgrading." He said part of his personal "upgrading" technique involved clothing — and that the suits he wore made him feel powerful. That resonated with me. My personal image is much more relaxed, and I almost never show up in a suit, but I do believe in dressing well. When I do put on a suit, I truly do feel stronger. Think about it: when you see a well-dressed woman or man, you get an immediate impression of who you believe them to be, and it's usually that of someone in some sort of power position. It goes back to what I mentioned earlier about appearances and first impressions.

When you ask yourself about external reputations, think about people like Tony Robbins, Tim Ferris, Tom Bilyeau, Brene Brown, Oprah Winfrey, and others who have achieved so much in this lifetime. Their success has to do with their constant struggle to understand, connect and move through. It doesn't mean they don't have their bad days; they've simply taken greater risks, and we reward them for it.

What do people love about Oprah? (Don't love Oprah? Then think of some other successful person you respect.) Do people love Oprah because she gave away cars on her show? Or is it because of her vulnerability — how early on in her talk show, she often cried with her audience? Tim Ferris wanted to commit suicide, but rose above the despair to become successful. Tony Robbins got sick and tired of having nothing material to show for himself. One day, after giving away the last of his tiny amount of money, he got a surprise envelope in the mail with cash from a friend who was finally paying him back. These are people just like you and me, the only difference being their determination to find a better way, to do more, to share and to connect with people on a largest possible scale. They did so by *creating for themselves* an external reputation.

I'm sorry to say that my reputation growing up was not the greatest. I wasn't the greatest friend, son or brother. I was cheap, self-centered, and didn't use foresight to see if my actions were going to positively or negatively affect those around me. I never want anyone that reads this book to think I was some angel or saint when I was younger — my external reputation far exceeded my small circle, and it *sucked*. It was a badge of dishonor that people would joke about around me. I can look back on it now and see it clearly, but at the time, although I cared, I didn't care enough to *change*. It wasn't until my external reputation started to cost me dearly that I finally realized it was time for change. There's no time like the present, but there's also no time like finally waking up and recognizing how you've really been living.

One time when I was attending a Tony Robbins *Unleash the Power Within* seminar, he spoke of how he had finally woken up and realized the "secret to living is giving," as he put it. When you give of yourself, give your heart, and sacrifice your own time and energy for the good of others, you can begin to reshape your external reputation. What's even more beautiful is that you can be forgiven as part of that process. You can forgive *yourself* — in fact, that's a necessary part of improving your internal reputation — and others who you may have wronged may find it in themselves to forgive you too. This journey of change for me began because I hit rock bottom emotionally and selfishly. It was the best thing that ever happened to me. I now have a yardstick of how far down I had gone, and now I feel like I'm going to run out of tape as I measure my personal and professional successes! Of course, these measurements aren't so I can stroke my own ego, but they serve as a tool, markers that ensure I am on the right path and can continue to work toward my goals along the journey of life.

As you focus on developing your external reputation, remember that all the "greats" were once just like you. And that means that you, too, can develop yourself to become the next Oprah, Tony Robbins, Tim Ferris, or whoever you want to be. You just have to get out of your own way, allow the process to happen, and don't give yourself any excuses. You can see how the internal and external reputation work hand in hand, right?

As you develop your work ethic, people will notice, and that adds to your external reputation. As you deal honestly with others, that adds to your external reputation, too. Your external reputation isn't just "smile, camera, action" when the camera's on; it's *who you are* when the camera is off, too. Character is what you do when nobody is looking — it's your *identity*. That identity is the core of your external reputation, and it can't be faked.

I teach about the importance of connecting with prospects on a personal level, so they can see us as well-rounded human beings, not cyborgs focused on setting the appointment or closing the deal. It's the nuts and bolts of how we build our external reputation.

In my business, I talk to so many people I don't know yet (I avoid the word *strangers*), so being personable and easy to talk to and professional is my focus. By the time I finish a conversation with a prospect, they've formed a vision of who they believe me to be, as I've exposed my character to them. I find out what their real estate world looks like, and I also get to know the human side of them. I dig into their life and way of living, and truly connect. Now, they don't know who I am at any reasonable depth, but what they feel is connected and understood. My external reputation is solidified in a positive way, upturning any negative preconceptions they may have had about what a real estate broker is like.

Δ Δ Δ

Let's recap Chapter 7 and see how important reputation is for our success:

• Reputation has two components that word together: *internal* and *external*.

• Your internal reputation is formed from your self-talk — that voice that either build you up or tears you down. Pay attention and listen to the voices — are they encouraging or discouraging? Does heeding them point you toward your goals or away from them? Embrace the good voice and discard the bad. This takes training and time. It requires a conscious effort.

• Your external reputation is just how it sounds: what others think of you. You can't fudge this; it has to be real and genuine. Show the world who you really want to be by appearing to have already reached that lofty goal.

• Apply the communication tools in the earlier chapters to help create that reputation!

CHAPTER 8

ROLE-PLAY CALL

Here's where the rubber meets the road! I want you to hear what it sounds like when we take all these communication secrets and roll them into one fluid conversation. Read the transcript and listen to the audio, and I'll show you how it's done.

If you're reading this in ebook format, click the link below to hear the actual audio as you're following along with the transcript. If you're reading a hard copy of this book, you can pull up the audio at www.coachingwithsteve.com/listennow. I want you to pay particular attention to cadence, tonality, rebuttals, and other approaches, and realize that every part of this conversation is strategic — nothing is left to chance. Listen to what it sounds like when you're *polished*.

Note: This example is geared at a real estate conversation, but the principles are the same no matter what your type of business. Consider how you can apply the techniques to your own conversations.

Role-play: A seller who wants to try selling their house without an agent

Steven: Ring, ring.

Nick: Hello.

Steven: Good morning. I'm looking for Nick, please.

Nick: This is Nick. Who's this?

Steven: Nick, this is Steven from over at Whissel Realty. You received a flyer in the mail and registered online just to get more information about your property. It looks like you were just playing around with that site. I was calling to see what does your real estate inquiry look like at the moment. What's going on with your housing needs, Nick?

Nick: My wife and I are thinking of moving. We were just playing around with the online calculator to see what our current home is worth. Very early stages though, but we're thinking of making a move.

Steven: The reason that you got that flyer in the mail is...Did you notice my listing that sold in like three seconds, that was about three blocks away? I already looked up your address. That was the one I had on 123 Main Street. Did you ever see that house and the open house we did, or did you simply get my flyer?

Nick: I got your flyer.

Steven: I'm assuming you're owning. That's the only people that would register on this site, just for value. Is that safe to say? You and your wife are owning your home currently?

Nick: Yeah, we are.

Steven: For my own information, Nick, what is your wife's name?

Nick: It's Emily.

Steven: Emily. When anybody starts to look at value, it makes me assume you're either just wanting to know where your place is in the market, or you're considering the sale of your home. Which is it for you?

Nick: We're definitely considering selling our home.

Steven: As you [laughs] noticed, the for sale sign went up. A sold sign went up immediately thereafter. There's really nothing else in a half mile radius. There's nothing in the area. That's the big reason that I put out the card because I've accumulated a number of buyers that are still looking in your area. When were you and Emily planning on putting your home on the market for sale, Nick?

Nick: Pretty soon. We're thinking of making a move here in the next — I don't know — maybe three, four months. Pretty soon.

Steven: Are you staying local? Are you moving out of state? What does your future look like for you?

Nick: We're going to stay in San Diego. We're going to move closer to the beach. Probably Ocean Beach or PB or something.

Steven: Cool. This property, we're in Oceanside right now. The type of property that I just sold was a four bedroom, three bath. Most of the houses in there are a fair size. What type of home are you currently living in?

Nick: It's around that same thing. We have four bedroom, two bathroom.

Steven: Is getting closer to the beach the only lifestyle change, or were you upsizing or downsizing? What type of home do you need out of your next property?

Nick: I don't know that we're upsizing or downsizing. We'd like maybe something similar. We're okay with three bedrooms. I think we just wanted to get a little more south.

Steven: The house that I just sold went for I think it was $22,000 over list. It was absolutely crazy. We just sold it at $610,000. That area is called a planned urban development. There's only five models in that area. It looks like you're literally two blocks away. Did you have the same home as that one, far as square footage and everything? Do you know if it was a model match, Nick? Was it the Bella Vista 2 plan in that area? Which one do you have of that four bedroom plan?

Nick: [laughs] I'm sorry. Can you repeat that?

Steven: Are you a model match? Is your home identical to the one that I just sold, or is yours a slight alteration of that one?

Nick: Yeah. It's a pretty close match. I think it's model match.

Steven: It's a model match. Are you planning on staying around the same price point when you move closer to the beach? It gets more expensive over there. I just want you to be completely aware of what you're looking for in that area.

Nick: Yeah. We're hoping to stay around the same price.

Steven: Because you're only three or four months away, which actually is really quick in the real estate world, have you spoken to a financial professional to make sure that you're absolutely ready for this, or you're planning on paying cash for your next purchase?

Nick: We haven't talked to anyone yet. We were referred to a couple lenders. We just haven't made the call yet. No, we're not going to be paying in cash.

Steven: Are you aware that you may have to be in a financial position...Of course, I don't know the full answer to this yet, but maybe you do. Do you have to sell your home before you can purchase your next home?

Nick: Yeah, I think we do.

Steven: When you make this entire transition, Nick, has there been a professional, someone like myself, that's having a real conversation with you, that's been aiding you or at least guiding you to what this whole process is going to look like?

Nick: No. We've gotten a couple calls and everything, but no, we don't really want to work with anyone. We want to list the home on our own.

Steven: In this particular market, it seems like that should be no big deal, right, to sell your home. Before I get into the complexities of what this market looks like, especially when it looks easy, when you sell your home, do you have a place to go in transition, or does it have to be a seamless I'm selling and I'm buying at the same time? Can you describe that to me?

Nick: No, we don't have somewhere to go. We haven't actually thought about that. We'll have to sell. Whatever home we buy, it'll have to be a seamless transition.

Steven: With respect to what you do for a living — of course, you know I'm in real estate — what do you do, Nick? What is your primary occupation?

Nick: I'm a business owner.

Steven: Okay, what type of business?

Nick: I own a bicycle shop in Oceanside. Does pretty well.

Steven: That's awesome. That's awesome. Which one is it? I'm not an avid cyclist, but every once in a while, I've got a blowout so I've got to true my tires.

Nick: [laughs]

Steven: I'm wondering if I've been to your shop. Which shop is yours in Oceanside?

Nick: It's Nick's Performance Bicycles on 123 Main Street. Have you been there?

Steven: Yeah. Definitely. Actually, I bought my daughter's bike over there. That's awesome.

Nick: Oh, great.

Steven: It seems like you're going to be commuting then [laughs] from Ocean Beach.

Nick: [laughs]

Steven: [laughs] That's awesome.

Nick: [laughs]

Steven: When somebody comes in and they have to true a tire or something like that, how simple is that for you to do?

Nick: Pretty simple for me.

Steven: I don't even have the tools to true a tire. If I did something like that, I'd probably put it so out of whack that I'd be in more trouble than I was in the first place. That's simply because you know exactly what you're doing and how simple that situation is to rectify. Would you agree?

Nick: Yeah, I'd agree with that.

Steven: The property I just mentioned that I sold a couple blocks away from you, I got them $22,000 over list. Do you think I did that with one offer?

Nick: No, probably more than that.

Steven: Exactly. Have you ever dealt with multiple offers before? You ever sold a home on your own?

Nick: No, we haven't.

Steven: Would you rather shortchange yourself, or would you rather make more money?

Nick: I want to make more money.

Steven: You know how to do that by selling your own home?

Nick: We figured by not paying an agent, that we'd be getting more money.

Steven: That's a great thought. It's a simple, mathematical, initial thought of "Hey, I'm going to save X," right?

Nick: Yeah.

Steven: Because you haven't worked with multiple offers before, vetted the purchasers on your property, got them to fight over your property, get them to pay more than appraised value, spoke to their lenders, negotiated repairs that they may request on your home once they do an inspection...
Here's the kicker. You're dealing with contract law. Are you familiar with any of that stuff or that type of pressure in a home environment when you're trying to sell your home?

Nick: No, but I thought that we could just pay an attorney to deal with the contracts.

Steven: Do you think an attorney is dealing with multiple buyers, or is he simply going to deal with the contract that you get because you chose the one that you thought was right for you?

Nick: Yeah, he's not going to deal with the offers. I thought we could handle that.

Steven: Exactly. All I'm trying to impress upon you is there's a different way. I've been at this for 22 years, Nick. I do it at a very high level. I'd love to send you my social proof so you can not only see the satisfaction of what my clients have to say after we've concluded the transaction, but what they've said about how the transaction goes. I'm not saying that you need to work with me. I'm saying that I want to offer you and Emily options. If the options that I present to you don't make financial sense, okay. I know I'd rather have options to consider instead of just pigeonholing myself and saying, "I know how to do this," because I don't. I don't know how to tune up a bike. I don't know how to true a tire. I don't know how simple certain things are. They become simple after you've done them dozens and dozens and dozens of times. I've done this over 1,500 times for my clients. When would be a good time to just sit down with you and Emily, look at your house, evaluate it properly, tell you what's really going on in the marketplace, and then presenting you what's called a net sheet, showing you what you believe the actual cost to you is versus what it will be? Are weekends better or evenings during the week? What works best for you, Nick?

Nick: Probably weekends.

Steven: Saturday or Sunday preferable to you?

Nick: Saturday.

Steven: Morning or afternoon?

Nick: Let's do morning.

Steven: Let's say 10:30 in the morning on Saturday. Your house did come. The address came across on the site that I'm calling you from. 234 Main Street in Oceanside. That is your current address, correct?

Nick: Yeah, it is.

Steven: This phone number, is this the best contact number for you?

Nick: Yup.

Steven: Nick@performancebicycles.com, that's the best email to reach you?

Nick: Yeah, that's the best email.

Steven: I'll send you some stuff by email after we conclude this call. Nick, I really appreciate you being incredibly open to everything that I've mentioned and suggested. Obviously, you're open to it on a bigger front because we are meeting. I'm glad that I can resonate some of the professionalism I mentioned that goes into helping the client in the end. Thank you for your time.

Nick: Thank you. Thanks for all the info.

Steven: Absolutely. I'll see you guys on Saturday at 10:30, okay?

Nick: Okay, sounds good.

Steven: All right. Be well.

Nick: All right. Bye.

Steven: Bye.

...

Nick: Wow.

Man: Nice. [laughs] What'd you think, Nick? [laughs]

Nick: Excuse my language. I literally feel like you brain f**ked me to the point where... [laughter]

Woman: Nick, trust me. He did.

Steven: [laughs]

Nick: It was like magic. It was really, really good. [laughs]

Steven: That's all good. [laughs]

Nick: I mean that in the best possible way. [laughs]

Steven: I understand. I punished you mentally to make you feel like if you didn't make an appointment with me, you are not a very smart individual.

Nick: You punished me. That's exactly what it was. [laughs] That was great.

Steven: That felt good.

Man: Boom.

Transcription by CastingWords

To get a step-by-step explanation, where I break down exactly what I did in that call and how I did it, I encourage you to head over to www.coachingwithsteve.com/learn, where I offer a more in-depth training in these techniques, so that *you* can become an expert yourself.

CHAPTER 9

PRACTICE PRACTICE PRACTICE

Practice

We all have the same opportunity in a given day to focus our attention on the things that intrigue us, excite us, and improve us. We each have 86,400 seconds, each and every day, and we can choose how to spend them — that is a choice that is within our power. Sure, some things you just have to do (sleep, eat, work, etc.), but there's always some amount of discretionary time, and that's where the rubber meets the road. We've all seen how the best athletes and musicians commit themselves to a disciplined practice regimen; if you want to excel in your own area of expertise, it's no different. Even the most gifted performers have to put in many hours of practice, and those who are most relentless in that pursuit of perfection are the ones that stand out and get the big contracts and accolades.

For the star athlete, practice doesn't just mean throwing a ball through a hoop over and over again (though that's part of it!) — it also means observing and acquiring knowledge. They study play books and watch hours of film on the opposing team's plays, going above and beyond, so that on game day, they have an edge. Consistency is key. Practice is work! It's not always fun — it can be painful and time consuming, but it can also be enlightening and blissful.

I would not have reached the point of success that I have in my career if I hadn't spent so much time on role play calls over the years. The practice I put in each and every one of those mornings reshaped me into the person I am today. The feedback I received allowed me to find a better way to deliver my message. Practice isn't just about mastering a move, practice allows you to see the whole field because you don't have to focus on what you don't know and get distracted with fumbling your way through. Practice helps you layer strength after strength, so you can become unstoppable and a force to be reckoned with in your particular field.

In the end, putting in the practice is up to us; but no learning, growing athlete, musician, or other professional gets there completely on their own. I got here thanks to hard work and the encouragement of my life coach, real estate coach, and fitness coach. They have pushed me and challenged me in ways — ways in which I wasn't able to push myself on my own. I think we have a natural "off" switch that activates when things get too challenging, and we need some external motivation to keep us going beyond our self-created limits. We could all benefit form a great mentor.

Practice

Practicing through role play has helped me to be able to anticipate any objection that may come while qualifying a prospect, and be able to handle it without missing a beat. When you've practiced LPMAMA enough times, you'll never find yourself lost in a qualifying conversation. You won't need to stumble through with, "Um, ah, you know." You'll have the answers and be able to continue forging that connection.

When you practice mirroring and matching techniques, so you can talk at your prospect's cadence, match their tonality, and posture yourself where you match their posture, you'll create that all-important rapport. Try working with an actual mirror to see how you show up and what your facial expressions and posture look like. Your reflection is free, so you have no reason not to do this unless you simply are afraid to begin your transformation. It's okay! Many of us are naturally intimidated by such a challenge, but I assure you that you can do it, and it's worth it.

Remember to use empowering language. It doesn't take rocket science to determine if you said something mean, distancing, offensive, or confusing. Review the empowering terms in Chapter 5 and get used to using them. You have the power to make people feel good about themselves, and give them hope and confidence — and you'll reap the rewards of that good deed!

When it comes to finding opportunity through physiology, just watch what happens to someone when they get happy, sad, mad, or indifferent. There are expressions that they show in their face or body, and tones they use in their voice. It's easy to practice recognizing these cues, because there are plenty of crowded areas where you can just people-watch, or just enjoy a movie or TV show while paying attention to those signs. See if you can tell what they're experiencing. The more often you do this, the more you'll recognize the signals when a prospect is telling you something through a physiological change versus the words they use. It makes a transaction so much more incredible when all parties share the same experience, and the only way to do this is by learning how to frame the entire experience using the tools we've introduced in this book.

Practice

I can't make you do anything; I can simply influence you and demonstrate to you why you should connect with people at a deeper level, and what the success will look like should you take on that challenge. I can't make you practice to become the best you can be; I can simply remind you that 95% of the population does just enough to get by, 5% crush it, and the top 1% of that 5% *dominate*. And it's no accident. The key is practice. Hard work. Determination. Loss, stress, and sleepless nights. Ten thousand hours of repetition. But also happiness, mentors, community support, and so much more. A relentless thirst for knowledge, and no fear of putting in the required time for success. No giving up when things take a downturn or go sideways.

The more you learn, the more you can apply. The more you apply, the more you'll create separation from the mediocre and find yourself among the best, and the best are always being challenged by those trying to dethrone them. See that as a sign of respect, not a threat, since people want to be more like you, as they see something good and admirable and inspiring in you.

Commit to moving out of your comfort zone and doing something unprecedented each week.

Don't resist the positive change in your life, just because it isn't easy. None of my success could have happened for me if I didn't practice religiously, so when you ask yourself what you're willing to do to take yourself to the next level, be honest with yourself and carve the time out to implement and execute your plan.

Nothing happens without a plan, and nothing happens without taking ownership in order to get it done. Nothing worth achieving comes overnight or comes easily. I know from firsthand experience that if you don't ask, you don't get. You must build off of your experiences and draw from your challenges, as these are what shape us.

I wish you an incredible journey in becoming a fantastic communicator!

Δ Δ Δ

Sources

[1]https://venturebeat.com/2015/03/27/why-businesses-cant-ignore-sms-hint-90-of-people-read-a-text-message-within-the-first-3-minutes/

[2]https://www.sbs.com.au/topics/life/culture/article/2017/02/06/psychologists-explain-your-phone-anxiety-and-how-get-over-it

[3]https://ourworldindata.org/literacy [back to reading]

[4]https://www.oecd-ilibrary.org/economics/how-was-life_9789264214262-en

[5]https://www.psychologytoday.com/us/blog/get-psyched/201207/learning-through-visuals

[6]https://www.dictionary.com/browse/sell?s=ts

[7]https://www.theguardian.com/science/2006/aug/23/usnews.internationalnews

[8]https://www.wired.com/2012/11/amy-cuddy-first-impressions/

[9]https://www.ncbi.nlm.nih.gov/pubmed/16866745

[10]https://www.16personalities.com/personality-types

ABOUT THE AUTHOR

Steven Wener is an award-winning residential real estate agent with 24 years of experience. Since 2014, he's been part of the #1 real estate team in San Diego, according to *The Wall Street Journal*, Zillow and Trulia. Steven has mastered the art of turning prospects into clients, and clients into raving fans! He's personally made tens of thousands of outbound cold calls and helped over 1,500 families with their real estate needs. Through this process, Steven has diligently studied initial engagement experiences and become a trusted source for professionals who want to improve their conversion rates.

Learn more at **http://coachingwithsteve.com**

This book is available in ebook, paperback, and audiobook formats.